X3   3/02

WHALES

Melissa and Brandon Cole

BLACKBIRCH PRESS, INC.

WOODBRIDGE, CONNECTICUT

Published by Blackbirch Press, Inc.
260 Amity Road
Woodbridge, CT 06525

Email: staff@blackbirch.com
Web site: www.blackbirch.com

©2001 by Blackbirch Press, Inc.
First Edition

Printed in China

Photo Credits: All images ©Brandon D. Cole, except pages 13, 21, 22: ©Melissa S. Cole

10 9 8 7 6 5 4 3 2 1

Library of Congress Cataloging-in-Publication Data
Cole, Melissa S.
Whales / by Melissa S. Cole.
    p.   cm. — (Wild marine animals!)
ISBN 1-56711-441-5 (hardcover: alk. paper)
1. Whales—Juvenile literature. [1. Whales.]   I. Title.
QL737.C4 C574   2001
599.5—dc21
                                                              2001001574

Contents

Introduction

This young sperm whale is 25 feet (7.6 meters) long. Sperm whales can grow to a length of 60 feet (18.2 meters).

More than 70 species of whales swim in the world's oceans today. Some whales live in warm, shallow, equatorial waters. Others feed in cold, deep, northern seas. Many species migrate, or travel, between the two.

Orcas, or killer whales, feed on fish, seals, dolphins, and sometimes other whales.

Many years ago, people thought that whales were fish. Today, we know that whales are mammals, like humans. Whales differ from fish in several ways. Whales don't have gills like fish do. Instead, they use their huge lungs to breathe. They are warm-blooded, not cold-blooded like fish. Instead of laying eggs, whales give birth to live babies and nurse them with milk. Long ago, people probably confused whales with fish because whales spend their entire lives in water.

Whales, dolphins, and porpoises belong to a group of marine mammals that scientists call cetaceans. Whales come in many shapes and sizes. Some whales are long and thin—built to glide swiftly through the ocean. Other whales are short and stocky. Some whales like to sing, while others prefer to grunt and whistle. Toothed whales have sharp, cone-shaped teeth for catching slippery fish and squid. Baleen whales don't have teeth at all. Instead, they have bristly, comb-like plates called baleen. Baleen strains small fish and shrimp-like krill out of the water. Many years ago, baleen was used in making women's clothing.

Following are a few of the world's most common types of whales.

The blue whale is the largest animal on Earth.

Blue Whales

The blue whale may be the largest animal ever to have lived on Earth. Its average length is 82 feet (25 meters), but lengths of more than 110 feet (33.5 meters) have been recorded. Blue whales are baleen whales that feed on krill. They are blue-gray in color and have a small dorsal fin located about three-quarters of the way down their backs. When a blue whale breathes, its blow (moist air forced out of the blowhole) can reach heights of 30 feet (9.1 meters). Blue whales are found in cold and temperate, or mild, waters worldwide.

Beluga Whales

Beluga whales are white. They usually grow to lengths of between 9 and 16 feet (2.7 and 4.8 meters). They are toothed whales that feed on fish and squid. Belugas are found in the cold, arctic waters near Russia, Greenland, and Canada. They are known as the "canaries of the sea" because they make many noises, such as squeaks, chirps, and whistles.

Beluga whales live in the cold waters of the Arctic Ocean.

Orca Whales

With their distinctive black-and-white coloration, orcas—also called killer whales—are easy to recognize. Adult orcas usually grow to lengths of between 18 and 32 feet (5.5 and 9.8 meters). Orcas belong to a group of whales, commonly called "blackfish," which includes pilot whales, melon-headed whales, and other toothed whales with black skin. Some orcas, called residents, stay close to shore and feed mainly on fish. Transient orcas roam the open seas in packs, feeding on a variety of sea animals, such as seals, dolphins, turtles, and even other whales.

Humpback Whales

Humpback whales are one of the most energetic whales. They often leap completely out of the water, called breaching, or wildly slap their huge pectoral fins or tail flukes (lobes) against the water's surface. They have knobby heads and long flippers. Adult humpback whales can be as long as 49 feet (15 meters). Each humpback whale has a unique black and white pattern on its flukes, similar to a human fingerprint. Because of this, scientists have been able to distinguish thousands of humpbacks.

Humpback whales often breach—they leap completely out of the water.

Southern Right Whales

Southern right whales are large, dark, baleen whales. Adults can grow to lengths of 36 to 59 feet (11 to 18 meters). These whales don't have dorsal fins, and their heads are covered with rough, white patches of skin called callosities.

Southern right whales can be found swimming off the coasts of North and South America. They have an endangered

Southern right whales have patches of rough skin, called callosities, on their heads.

cousin called the northern right whale. There are only about 300 northern right whales in the world's oceans today.

Gray Whales

Gray whales are one of the most well known types of whales. Many people have had a chance to watch from shore or in boats as gray whales migrate more than 12,000 miles (19,355 kilometers) each year. The creatures move from their arctic feeding grounds to the warm waters near Baja, Mexico, where they breed and give birth to their young. Adults reach lengths between 39 and 46 feet (11.9 and 14 meters).

The Body of a Whale

Whales live their entire lives in water. They have long, sleek, almost hairless bodies. A whale's flippers tuck in at its side, which allows it to cruise through the water with ease.

Female baleen whales are usually larger than males. In toothed whales, the males have larger bodies.

A whale's tail flukes, which are wide and strong, propel it forward with an up-and-down motion, instead of a side-to-side movement like a fish. A blow from a tail fluke can keep enemies such as sharks, other whales, and even human hunters, away.

Whales use their back, or dorsal, fins to maintain their stability in the water as they swim. A whale's sex organs and mammary (milk) glands are tucked up inside, so its body remains smooth and streamlined. Blowholes, which function like human nostrils, are located at the top of a whale's head. This allows a whale to take a deep breath without having to lift its heavy head out of the water.

Baleen whales, like the gray whale, have twin blowholes.

Whales can breathe only through their blowholes—not their mouths. Toothed whales usually have a single blowhole, while baleen whales have two.

When a whale breathes, air exits the blowhole with such force that it blows the water on top of the whale's head into the air. This warm air condenses in the cool air above the whale and forms a misty cloud called a blow.

Beneath a whale's skin is a thick layer of fat, or blubber. Blubber helps whales float. It also allows whales to stay warm in water since they don't have thick fur coats like many other mammals.

A whale's tail fluke moves in an up-and-down motion to move it forward.

Special Features

Even though most whales have good eyesight, they are not able to see very far in murky water. A special ability, called echolocation, helps them navigate without sight. Whales have many air sacs inside their heads. A whale can squeeze air from one air sac to another, which makes a lot of noise. The whale can then send these noises into the water, where they form sound waves. When the sound waves hit something—such as a boat or a fish—they bounce back to the whale. The whale can then form a "sound picture" and know what lies ahead. Toothed whales usually have a better sense of echolocation than baleen whales. Some whales, such as the sperm whale, can send sound waves strong enough to stun or kill their prey.

A baby southern right whale looks at the camera. Most whales have good eyesight.

Hunting

Baleen whales have long, curved upper jaws that hold their plates of baleen. Baleen plates are like stiff, wiry bristle brushes hanging from a whale's top jaw. These plates filter fish, krill, and plankton from the sea. The size and shape of baleen plates varies from species to species, depending on what the whale eats. Some whales, such as the blue whale, swim along with their mouths slightly open. In a good feeding area, the water will be filled with fish or krill that are swept into the whale's open mouth. When the whale is ready to swallow, it pushes its huge tongue to the roof of its mouth. Water flows out between the bristly baleen plates, but tiny fish are trapped inside.

Humpback whales often feed in a group. They work together as a team, sometimes blowing bubbles to make their own "fishing nets." The group begins by swimming in a circle beneath a school of fish or krill. The whales then blow a steady stream of bubbles from their blowholes. As the bubbles rise, they form a kind of net that traps the prey inside.

Baleen plates are bristle-like brushes used to strain food from the sea.

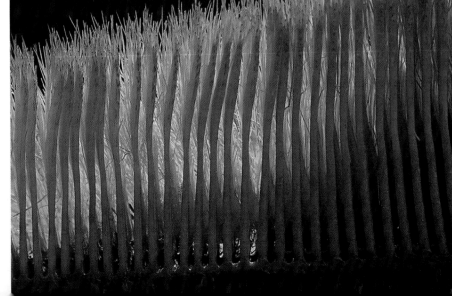

Next, the whales charge through the center toward the surface with their mouths wide open. They end up with thousands of gallons of water in their pleated, balloon-like throats, along with a mouthful of food. This technique is called lunge feeding, or bubble-net feeding. Humpbacks can do this alone, but are more successful if they work as a group.

Toothed whales such as beluga, orca, and sperm whales have large cone-shaped teeth. Most toothed whales do not need to chew their food. They simply grasp their slippery prey, usually fish or squid, with their sharp teeth and swallow it whole!

Below left: Orcas, like other toothed whales, have cone-shaped teeth.
Below right: A humpback whale surfaces with a mouthful of fish and water
Opposite: Sperm whales can stay under water for more than two hours.

Sperm whales are some of the most amazing eaters in the ocean. Scientists once found a sperm whale with 28,000 undigested squid inside its stomach, along with a man's boot and a large rock. Sperm whales sometimes feed on giant squid. These squid can be very large and strong, sometimes growing to more than 65 feet (19.8 meters) in length. When searching for prey, sperm whales can dive to more than 2 miles (3.2 kilometers) below the ocean surface and can stay under for more than two hours.

Social Life

A "nursery school" of female sperm whales and their young communicate through clicking sounds.

Feeding is the single most important factor in whale societies. The biggest differences occur between baleen whales and toothed whales. Toothed whales live everywhere—from deep, polar oceans to warm rivers and estuaries near the equator. They may form groups of only a few whales, as well as groups of more than 1,000 whales, called pods.

Sperm whales form groups called "nursery schools" made up of females and babies, called calves. When young males in the group are between the ages of seven to ten years, they leave the "nursery school" and join other young males in groups called "bachelor schools." When males are about 27 years old and physically mature, they compete against other males for food and mates.

All whales have a sense called biomagnetism that enables them to follow Earth's magnetic field, sort of like a compass. Because Earth's magnetic field is always changing, whales may not be aware of exactly where they are headed. If they follow the wrong route, it can lead them toward shore.

Every year, thousands of whales are found stranded, alive or dead, on beaches all over the world. Pilot whales are more easily stranded than other whales. Their social bonds are so strong that they won't leave each other behind, even when just one animal is stranded.

Baleen whales usually don't form permanent groups and are less likely to become stranded. Most baleen whales feed in the rich waters of Alaska and the poles in the summer. They then migrate to warm tropical waters to mate and give birth to their young.

Whales use a variety of sounds to communicate. They sing, moan, creak, buzz, click, and snap—filling the sea with their signals. At certain depths their sounds can travel hundreds of miles.

Southern right whales like these migrate thousands of miles each year.

The Mating Game

Left: A group of male belugas follows a female.
Above: Whales, like these southern right whales, splash a lot during courtship.

Because whales spend most of their lives below the water's surface, little is known about their mating behavior. Scientists do know that whales often breed in late winter or early spring. Females begin breeding when they are five to six years old. They are pregnant for about twelve months.

Sometimes, many males follow a single female, and often she will mate with more than one male. Humpbacks are famous for their love songs, which form some of the longest and most complex songs in the animal kingdom. Although they can occur at any time, many unusual behaviors, such as breaching, are seen during breeding season. Breaching occurs when whales leap completely out of the water and land with a monstrous splash. Spyhopping is the name used to describe the behavior when whales push their bodies partially out of the water and take a look around them.

Occasionally whales hang with their heads below the surface and their tails up in the air, swinging back and forth, slapping the water. This is known as lob tailing. No one really knows why whales perform these behaviors.

A playful orca cartwheels through the water.

Raising Young

Many types of whales, such as gray whales and humpbacks, migrate to warmer areas of the world to give birth to their young. Baby whales have very little blubber to keep them warm and help them float. They need to be born in warm water, where they have a chance to feed and grow strong.

A newborn humpback stays close to its mother.

Babies are usually born tail first. The mother will often twist her body to break the umbilical cord. The mother, and often an assisting female—called an "aunt"—will then help the calf to the surface so it can take its first breath. Baby whales drink between 30 and 100 gallons of milk every day. Whale milk is extremely rich in fat and as thick as toothpaste.

A baby gray whale rests its chin on its mother.

Calves grow very quickly. Blue whale calves can gain as much as 9 pounds (4 kilograms) in weight every hour. A blue whale calf is about 20 feet (6.1 meters) long when it is born. After seven months, the whale reaches a length of 50 feet (15.2 meters)—two-thirds the size of its mother!

When baby gray whales are about two months old, they set out with their mothers on a long journey north. They often hitch a ride on their mother's back. By sticking close to her, a calf is pulled along in the water current created by her enormous body. This is very helpful, because gray whales have to travel more than 6,000 miles (9,677 kilometers) to get back to their arctic feeding grounds.

Baby whales usually stay with their mothers for two to three years. In orca and pilot whale societies, however, young whales live with their mothers for their entire lives.

Whales and Humans

Humans have hunted whales for centuries for food, oil, and baleen. Right whales were one of the first targets of large whaling ships. These whales were the "right" whales to hunt, because they were easy to approach, swam slowly, lived close to shore, floated when dead, and provided large quantities of meat, oil, and baleen. As their numbers decreased, hunters went after sperm whales. The quick and powerful blue whale was too fast for whalers until the late 1800's, when explosive harpoons and swift, steam-driven ships were invented. By the twentieth century, most of the great whales had been hunted almost to extinction.

Today, most countries have stopped hunting whales. Most people don't eat whale meat or blubber and many products have been invented to replace whalebone, baleen, and oil. Only a few countries, including Japan, Norway, Russia and Korea, still hunt whales, mainly for food.

Whale watchers greet a gray whale.

Today, one of the greatest dangers whales face is ocean pollution. Many chemicals, such as pesticides, oils, and sewage are dumped into the ocean. These poisons can seep into whale tissue and cause illness. A mother whale can pass these poisons to her newborn through her milk, causing the baby to become sick or even die.

Many people today have joined conservation groups that work to save whales. Some populations of whales, such as the gray whales, have increased. Scientists now believe there are as many gray whales as there were before people began hunting them. Guidelines are now enforced by the National Marine Fisheries Service (NMFS) to keep people from getting too close to whales without a special permit. In many areas of the world, marine parks have been set aside for the protection of whales. In these areas, whales can mate and give birth to young without the threat of hunters.

Whales are awe-inspiring, incredible animals. If we want to continue to share our planet with them, we need to protect these mysterious creatures and the oceans in which they live.

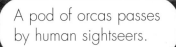

A pod of orcas passes by human sightseers.

23

GLOSSARY

blubber The fat under the skin of a whale.

endangered A plant or animal that is in danger of becoming extinct.

flippers Flat limbs on a sea creature that help it swim.

harpoon A long spear with an attached rope that can be thrown out of a special gun.

migrate To travel when seasons change.

prey An animal that is hunted by another animal for food.

FOR MORE INFORMATION

Books

Carwardine, Mark. *Killer Whale* (Natural World). Chatham, NJ: Raintree/Steck Vaughn, 1999.

Crewe, Sabrina. *The Whale* (Life Cycles). Chatham, NJ: Raintree/Steck Vaughn, 1997.

Dudley, Karen. *Blue Whales* (The Untamed World). Chatham, NJ: Raintree/Steck Vaughn, 1998.

LeBloas, Renee. *The Orca: Admiral of the Sea* (Close-Up). Watertown, MA: Charlesbridge Publishing, 2001.

Web Site

Baleen Whales

Find more information about baleen whales and their habitats—

www.seaworld.org/baleen_whales.html

INDEX